Why Horses Are...

Dream Big!

Written By Tana Thompson
Illustrated By Debbie Lentz

To: The Nelson Family, Always Follow Your Heart! 3/26/16

Kendall Neff Publishing

Carpenter's Son Publishing

a **FOUR DAYS LATE** project
of Kendall Neff Publishing
www.KendallNeff.com

The horse's mane stood straight out in the wind and shone like liquid gold in the sun that was setting over Marianna's left shoulder.

"Waaaaaaahoooooooooooo!" yelled Marianna. "We're flying!"

When her dad gave her the horse, he said, "That white mark on his face looks like a leap of fire." At seven, Marianna fell in love on the spot, named him Blaze, and then stayed madly in love with him for these past three years.

Outside the barn, Marianna let Blaze have a drink from the trough.

Inside the barn, she leaned against his golden side as she curried him. His wonderful horsey smell filled her head.

Before going into the house for the night, she patted his nose. It felt even softer than her red velvet Christmas dress. She hugged his neck a long time and said what she said every time she left him, "I'll love you forever."

The next day at lunch, Marianna sat with her friend Katie and talked about their horses.

Katie said, "I saw this place where horses help kids with special needs.

One of their horses is real sick.

They need another horse so more of the kids can ride.

Riding helps the kids—their rides are not just for fun like ours."

"I don't know what I'd ever do if couldn't ride Blaze," said Marianna.

Pharaoh

Speedy

Masterpiece

Masterpiece's Heir

Sandy

For the rest of the day, Marianna thought about horses, her horse,
and kids who had no horse.

The next morning, Marianna told her parents about the special horses and asked to visit them.

When they arrived, a volunteer gave Marianna and her parents a tour.

Outside, they saw beautiful pastures where horses could run or graze when they weren't working.

They visited the big barn and saw lots of horses, some ponies, and even the barn cat.

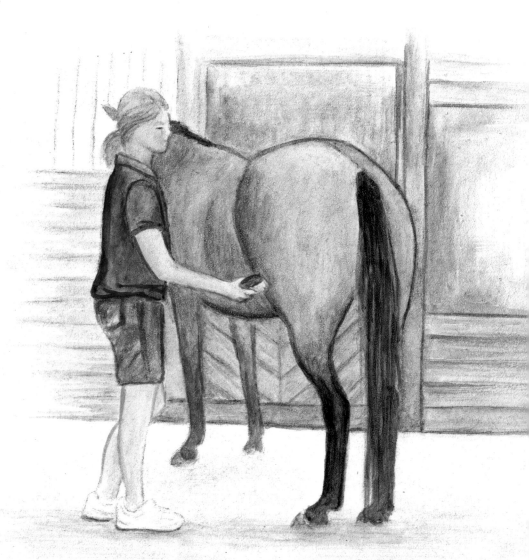

They watched as students with hearing problems learned to groom and tack a horse.

Students with seeing problems used touch to measure food. Students in wheelchairs fed horses through a low feeding station.

They walked into the huge riding arena
with its soft floor, smelling of sawdust.

A volunteer led a blind child to the mounting station. The horse gently brushed her leg as if to say, "Don't worry. I'll take care of you."

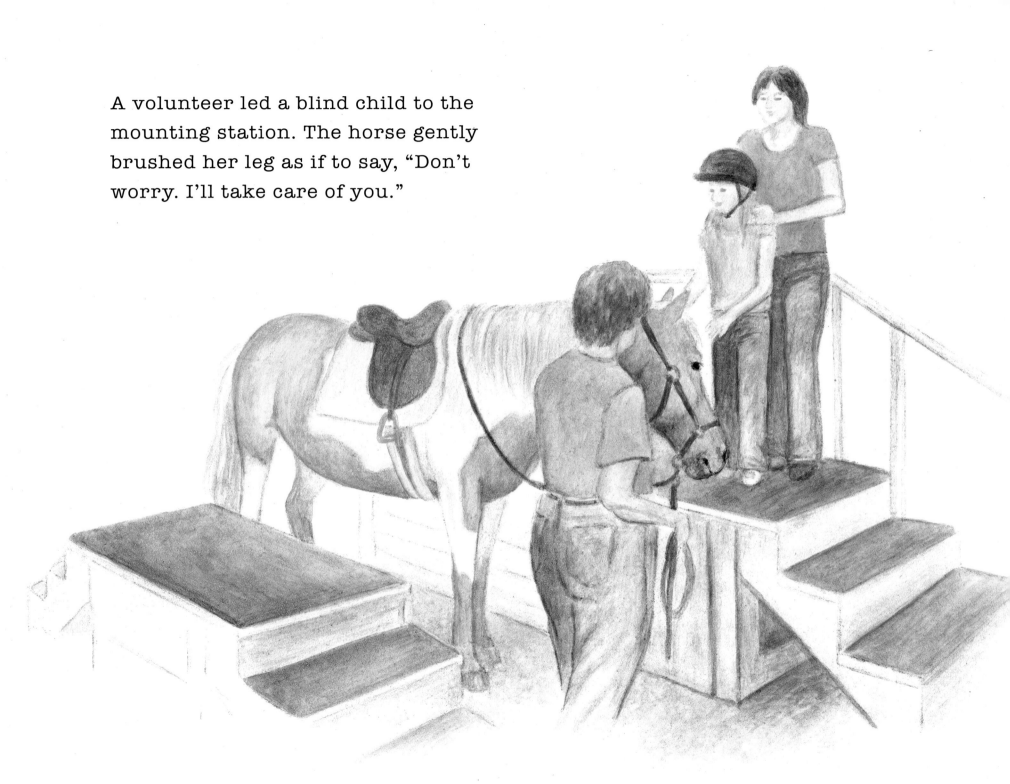

Everywhere she looked, Marianna saw children either chatting with their sidewalkers, whispering into horses' ears, or hugging horses' necks.

The volunteer said, "We are down one horse right now, so not all the kids can ride. For many of these children, riding is the only exercise they get. People offer us horses, but we can't take just any horse. Our horses have to be calm, safe, and trustworthy."

"Look over there. Tracey uses a wheelchair. At first, the horses scared her. To look at her now, sitting so straight and tall, you wouldn't know she needs a wheelchair."

Just then, Tracey urged her horse to go faster than she ever had. She called out to her teacher, "Look, I can run!"

Marianna thought about all her joy running with her safe and trustworthy Blaze. It was magic. It felt like soaring through the air. Like flying. Like she could go anywhere or do anything.

She was quiet all the way home.

In the barn, she leaned her head on Blaze's side and sobbed,

"Blaze, I think I should give you to that special barn so you can help other kids.

But how can I? I love you so much!!!"

Blaze turned his head and nuzzled her with his velvet nose. He looked at her with his soft, brown eyes. She was sure he understood.

She wrapped her arms around his neck for a long, long time.

Marianna now volunteers at the special barn. When she gets there, she always visits Blaze in his new stall. Each time, she leans against his golden side, smells his horsey smell, strokes his velvet nose.

She always says, "I'll love you forever."

The Story behind the story...

How the Marianna Greene Henry Special Equestrians (MGHSE) came into existence as a thriving program that daily produces miracles, magic and joys all started because one very special young woman had a dream and acted on it. Her story came to an abrupt end, but her family continued to turn her dream into a reality. In its 25-year history, many students with disabilities have come through its barn doors and exited the arena with more confidence in their future.

Marianna loved horses and helping kids. She had a special heart for children with disabilities. She convinced her parents to open a therapeutic riding program on their farm near the Alabama Institute for Deaf and Blind. Marianna died suddenly, and never saw her dream fulfilled. The Greene family wanted to honor her memory and initiated a pilot program with 8 students, a few horses, and professional and volunteer assistance.

Twenty-five years later, MGHSE has an average of 15 horses in its stalls. It annually serves anywhere from 350 to 400 children with disabilities. These facilities and programs have received national recognition professionally (PATH International) and in the media (National Geographic and People magazines).

Volunteers are at the heart of the programs as it takes many committed and reliable individuals to help make the opportunity available to so many children. The volunteers report they experienced more joy and magic than the kids might have, observing how riding a horse can change a child's anticipation of achievement.

Benefits of hippotherapy are many, including getting exercise for core body muscles. This is especially important to a wheelchair-bound child.

Marianna started a dream and her loving family finished it for her—for thousands of students over the years, it was, and is, literally a dream come true. It only takes one person to start a dream.

So, dream BIG, and unleash YOUR love!

See www.WhyHorsesAre.com for more of this story. Information also taken from many sources that include www.MGHArena.com, www.AIDB.org, reprints from The Daily Home's Jonathan Grass reporting, Mr. Pat Greene's promotional materials.

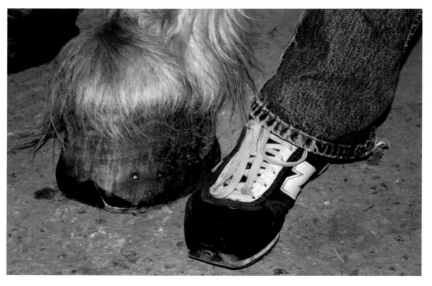

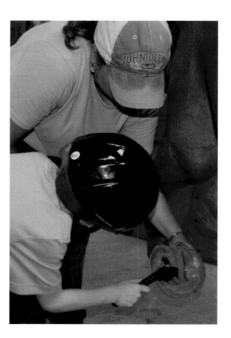

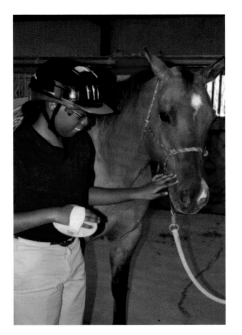

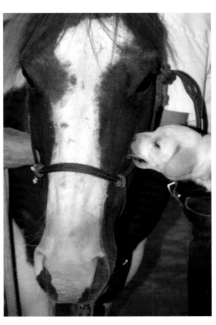

Marianna and Buttercup

Author: Tana Thompson

Illustrator: Debbie Lentz

Copy Editor: Audrey Owen, www.WritersHelper.com

Layout/Design: Suzanne Lawing

Marketing/PR: Cheryl Monkhouse

Website: Tim Monkhouse, Kathy Culler

Special Efforts: Adrienne A. Isakovic, Shirley Hamer,
                 The Dunklin Family

Publisher's Cataloging-in-Publication data

Thompson, Tana.

   Why Horses Are…/ written by Tana Thompson ;
   illustrated by Debbie Lentz.
   p. cm.
   ISBN 978-0-9891624-1-8
   Summary : Sharing her beloved horse with a horse
therapy program for kids with disabilities teaches a
young girl that love shared can inspire and benefit others.

[1. Horses--Fiction. 2. Horsemanship --Therapeutic
use --Fiction. 3. Horses --Therapeutic use --Fiction. 4.
Human-animal relationships –Fiction.] I. Lentz, Debbie.
II. Title.

PZ7.T3814 Wh 2013

[E] --dc23

ISBN: 978-0-9891624-1-8

Library of Congress Control Number: 2013905697

Kendall Neff Publishing in association with
Carpenter's Son Publishing

256.368.1559

Publr@KendallNeff.com

www.KendallNeff.com

100% of the Net Profits from the sale of this book
are given to charities and organizations that support
animals and their interactions with individuals,
organizations, and situations.
See our website www.WhyHorsesAre.com for a list
of recipients.

This book is available at cost to charitable and volunteer organizations (at the discretion of the Publisher) which would like to use it for fund-raising
purposes. Contact the publisher for details.
Publr@KendallNeff.com

Check our website www.WhyHorsesAre.com for
feature articles, blogs, stories, reviews and activities.
Share your favorite "horse" charities for consider-
ation to receive proceeds donations, and check out
our horse "stuff" at www.LoveUnleashed.us.